Study Guide for Case Transfer

Flaca Alexis-Dalce

Introduction

Marie Wislene Alexis, born on July 22, 1979, in Port-au-Prince, Haiti, faced early challenges when my parents left me in the care of her grandmother(Margeritte Paul) at three months old. At age 10, my mother sent for me to come to the United States, where she arrived without legal documentation. Despite these challenges, she graduated from high school, though her undocumented status initially prevented her from attending college.

Understanding firsthand the struggles of living without documentation, especially with family back in Haiti depending on her, Flaca's determination led her to pursue higher education once she obtained her Green Card. And become US-Citizen and I changed my name to Flaca Alexis- Dalce She studied Health Information Management at Keiser University, earning an associate degree, followed by a bachelor's degree in Business Management. She also pursued paralegal studies, becoming both a Paralegal and an Immigration Consultant.

Driven by her passion for helping others, Flaca continued her education, earning a second bachelor's degree in Human Resources Management and, in 2020, a Master's degree in Human Resources Management. She is a Certified Human Resources professional with 17 years of experience.

In June 2011, Flaca opened her first office, dedicating her career to assisting over 1,000 clients with immigration documentation and business consulting. She also teaches entrepreneurs how to manage and grow their businesses. Flaca emphasizes honesty and integrity in her work, reminding clients that, as a form preparer, she is there to help them achieve their dreams, not to provide le

I have been in this business for almost 14 years, dedicating my efforts to helping families reunite, especially given the challenges we face in the world today.

This Study Guidebook is designed to help you secure faster interviews at the U.S. Embassy. I have extensive experience and expertise in Immigration Documentation and Case approval, and I am confident that by following the steps outlined in this guide, you will achieve your goals.

Please read through each step carefully, and trust in the process. Your success is my priority.

Guide on Transferring Cases from the National Visa Center

This book is an essential resource that will teach you how to transfer cases from the National Visa Center. Please read the book step by step, as it provides all the necessary tools and information to navigate the process effectively. Typically, the transfer process takes 7-9 months, though it can sometimes be completed sooner.

Case Information

- Case Number: [Insert Case Number]
- Invoice Number: [Insert Invoice Number]
- Type of Visa: [Insert Type of Visa]

Petitioner Information

- Name: [Insert Petitioner Name]
- Email Address: [Insert Petitioner Email]
- Telephone Number: [Insert Petitioner Telephone Number]

Beneficiary Information

- Name: [Insert Beneficiary Name]
- Email Address: [Insert Beneficiary Email]
- Telephone Number: [Insert Beneficiary Telephone Number]

Next Steps

1. Send the Inquiry for Transfer: Ensure that the inquiry for the transfer is sent after confirming that the case is ready for the interview and all the files have been accepted.

Here's a breakdown of some of the popular visa categories and their purposes:

Popular Visa Categories

1. B-1 (Business Visitor)

   - Purpose: For individuals visiting the U.S. temporarily for business activities.
   - Required Before Applying: None

2. B-2 (Tourism, Vacation, Medical Treatment Visitor)

   - Purpose: For individuals visiting the U.S. for tourism, vacations, or medical treatment.
   - Required Before Applying: None

3. J (Exchange Visitor)

   - Purpose: For individuals participating in an exchange program, including au pairs, scholars, and physicians.
   - Required Before Applying: SEVIS (Student and Exchange Visitor Information System)

4. H-1B (Specialty Occupations)

   - Purpose: For professionals working in specialty occupations requiring highly specialized knowledge.
   - Required Before Applying: DOL (Department of Labor) certification, then USCIS (U.S. Citizenship and Immigration Services)

5. H-2A (Temporary Agricultural Worker)

   - Purpose: For temporary or seasonal agricultural work.
   - Required Before Applying: DOL certification, then USCIS

6. H-2B (Temporary Non-Agricultural Worker)

   - Purpose: For temporary non-agricultural work.
   - Required Before Applying: DOL certification, then USCIS

7. L (Intra-company Transferee)

- Purpose: For employees of an international company being transferred to a U.S. office.
- Required Before Applying: USCIS

8. O (Individuals with Extraordinary Ability)

- Purpose: For individuals with extraordinary abilities in sciences, arts, education, business, or athletics.
- Required Before Applying: USCIS

9. P (Performing Artists, Athletes, Entertainers)

- Purpose: For performers, artists, and athletes who are internationally recognized.
- Required Before Applying: USCIS

10. F/M (Student Visas)

- Purpose: For students attending academic or vocational schools.
- Required Before Applying: SEVIS

11. E (Treaty Trader/Investor)

- Purpose: For individuals who invest a substantial amount of capital in a U.S. business or engage in substantial trade with the U.S.
- Required Before Applying: None

12. U (Victim of Criminal Activity)

- Purpose: For victims of certain crimes who have suffered mental or physical abuse and are helpful to law enforcement.
- Required Before Applying: USCIS

13. T (Victim of Human Trafficking)

- Purpose: For victims of human trafficking.
- Required Before Applying: USCIS

14. TN/TD (NAFTA Professional Worker)

- Purpose: For professional workers from Mexico and Canada under the North American Free Trade Agreement (NAFTA).
- Required Before Applying: None

15. E-3 (Australian Professional Specialty)

- Purpose: For Australian nationals coming to the U.S. to work in a specialty occupation.
- Required Before Applying: DOL certification

When processing a case, ensure that you note the priority date and double-check the type of visa that applies to the case. This information will be crucial when sending the inquiry for transfer or preparing for the interview stage.

Immediate Relative & Family Sponsored Visas

1. Spouse of a U.S. Citizen
   - Visa Categories: IR1, CR1
2. Spouse of a U.S. Citizen Awaiting Approval of an I-130 Immigrant Petition
   - Visa Category: K-3
3. Fiancé(e) to Marry U.S. Citizen & Live in U.S.
   - Visa Category: K-1
4. Intercountry Adoption of Orphan Children by U.S. Citizens
   - Visa Categories: IR3, IH3, IR4, IH4
5. Certain Family Members of U.S. Citizens
   - Visa Categories: IR2, CR2, IR5, F1, F3, F4
6. Certain Family Members of Lawful Permanent Residents
   - Visa Categories: F2A, F2B

Employer Sponsored – Employment-Based Immigrants

1. Employment-Based Immigrants (Preference Groups):

    - Priority Workers [First]
    - Visa Category: E1

    - Professionals Holding Advanced Degrees and Persons of Exceptional Ability [Second]
    - Visa Category: E2

    - Professionals and Other Workers [Third]
    - Visa Categories: E3, EW3

    - Employment Creation/Investors [Fifth]
    - Visa Categories: C5, T5, R5, I5

    - Certain Special Immigrants [Fourth]
    - Visa Category: S (many)

2. Religious Workers

    - Visa Categories: SD, SR

3. Iraqi and Afghan Translators/Interpreters

    - Visa Category: SI

4. Iraqis Who Worked for/on Behalf of the U.S. Government

    - Visa Category: SQ

5. Afghans Who Worked for/on Behalf of the U.S. Government

    - Visa Category: SQ

Other Immigrants

1. Diversity Immigrant Visa

   - Visa Category: DV

2. Returning Resident

   - Visa Category: SB

Important Notes:

- K Visas: Although technically nonimmigrant visas, they are included here because they are for immigration-related purposes.
- Comprehensive List: The chart provided above is a list of many immigrant visa categories but does not cover every category. For a full listing of all immigrant visa categories, refer to the Foreign Affairs Manual, 9 FAM 502.1.

This information can help in identifying the correct visa category when processing cases, ensuring that the priority date and visa type are accurately recorded and that any necessary follow-up actions are taken accordingly.

All the U.S. Embassy information and contact details have been noted. Remember to always CC your clients when writing to the U.S. Embassy to request a transfer.

Address information

1)U.S. Embassy in Haiti
Tabarre 41
Route de Tabarre
Port-au-Prince, Haiti
Phone: 011-509-2229-8000
After-Hour Emergencies involving U.S. Citizens 509-2229-8000
Email: acspap@state.gov

2) U.S. EMBASSY IN THE DOMINICAN REPUBLIC
ADDRESS:
Av. Republica de Colombia 57
Santo Domingo
Dominican Republic
Phone: (809) 567-7775

3) U.S. Embassy in Nassaumap pin
ADDRESS:
42 Queen Street
Nassau, The Bahamas
HOURS OF OPERATION:
Closed
PHONE:
(242) 322-1181 ext. 0
EMAIL:
acsnassau@state.gov

4) U.S. EMBASSY Brazil
U.S. Embassy Brasília
SES - Av. das Nações, Quadra 801, Lote 03
70403-900 - Brasília, DF
Phone: (55-61) 3312-7000
Fax: (55-61) 3225-9136

5) U.S. Embassy in Chile
Av. Andrés Bello 2800
Las Condes
Santiago, Chile
Phone: (56-2) 2330-3000

6) U.S. Embassy in Mexico Citymap pin
ADDRESS:
Paseo de la Reforma 305
Colonia Cuauhtemoc
06500 Mexico, CDMX
PHONE:
(55) 5080-2000

Here's a template for the first letter requesting the transfer of a case:

[Your Name]
[Your Address]
[City, State, ZIP Code]
[Email Address]
[Phone Number]
[Date]

U.S. Embassy [Location]
[Embassy Address]

National Visa Center
31 Rochester Ave.
Portsmouth, NH 03801-2909

Subject: Request for Case Transfer - [Case Number]

Dear Sir/Madam,

I hope this letter finds you well. I am writing to formally request the transfer of the following immigration case to the appropriate U.S. Embassy. Below are the details of the case:

- Case Number: [Insert Case Number]
- Invoice Number: [Insert Invoice Number]
- Petitioner Name: [Insert Petitioner Name]
- Beneficiary Name: [Insert Beneficiary Name]
- Type of Visa: [Insert Visa Type]
- Priority Date: [Insert Priority Date]

Given that all required documents have been submitted and the case is now ready for an interview, I kindly request that the case be transferred to the U.S. Embassy in [Location] for further processing.

Please find the petitioner's and beneficiary's contact details below for your records:

Petitioner Information:

- Email: [Petitioner Email]
- Phone: [Petitioner Phone]

Beneficiary Information:

- Email: [Beneficiary Email]
- Phone: [Beneficiary Phone]

Please CC both the petitioner and beneficiary in all future correspondence.

Thank you for your prompt attention to this matter. Should you require any additional information, please do not hesitate to contact me.

Sincerely,

[Your Name]
[Your Title, if applicable]

[Your Name]
[Your Address]
[City, State, ZIP Code]
[Email Address]
[Phone Number]
[Date]

To Whom It May Concern,

I am writing to request the transfer of my immigration case due to urgent and concerning circumstances. My priority date is [Insert Priority Date].

The beneficiary of this case, [Insert Beneficiary's Name], is no longer residing in Haiti due to the severe insecurity, including incidents of kidnapping and violence, which have made it unsafe for anyone to remain. The situation in Haiti has deteriorated to the point where access to basic necessities, such as drinking water and food, is severely limited, and the overall environment is no longer suitable for my fiancé(e)/spouse.

Given these dire conditions, I am urgently requesting that the case be transferred to a safer location. I have included all the necessary documents for your review to facilitate this process.

Please consider this request with the utmost urgency, as the current situation poses a significant threat to the well-being of my fiancé(e)/spouse.

Thank you for your attention to this matter. I look forward to your prompt response.

Sincerely,

[Your Name]
[Your Title, if applicable]

Fingerprints

During the visa process an ink-free, digital fingerprint scan will be quickly taken. All nonimmigrant visa applicants ages 14 to 79 must be fingerprinted, and all immigrant visa (IV) applicants ages 14 and above must be fingerprinted.

There are some applicants whose fingerprints are not required, including:

- Applicants traveling on official government business, except for A-3 and G-5
- Applicants under age 14 or age 80 and over

Here's a summary of the key points from the Public Inquiry Form information:

Public Inquiry Form and Response Time

- Inquiry Response Time: NVC's response times to public inquiries are currently lengthy. It is recommended to submit a follow-up inquiry only if you do not receive a response within the published timeframes.

Interviews

- Scheduling Process: The U.S. Embassy or Consulate informs the NVC of available interview dates.
- Appointment Scheduling: NVC schedules interviews on a first-come, first-served basis. It's not possible to predict when an interview will be scheduled.
- Case Management: Once your case is complete, it will remain at NVC until an interview appointment is scheduled. NVC will then send the case to the appropriate U.S. Embassy or Consulate and notify the applicant, petitioner, and attorney (if applicable).

Case Status

- How to Check: For the most status of your case, you should log into the Consular Electronic Application Center (CEAC).

Last Contact Date

- Updating Information: To update the last contact date for cases actively processing at NVC, continue to pay fees and submit required documents via the CEAC.

Here's a summary of the current case file creation process and important steps to follow:

Current Case File Creation Time

- Timeframe: As of August 19, 2024, NVC is processing cases received from USCIS on August 14, 2024.

Process Overview

1. Case Creation: After USCIS sends your I-797 approval notice, they will forward your approved petition to the National Visa Center (NVC) for processing.
2. Data Entry: NVC will create your visa case and enter the necessary data from your petition into their system.
3. Welcome Letter: Once your case is created, NVC will send you a Welcome Letter that includes your Case Number and Invoice ID.

Important Actions

- Welcome Letter: Keep your Welcome Letter in a safe place, as you will need this information to log into the Consular Electronic Application Center (CEAC) throughout the entire visa process.
- Prepare Documents: During this time, review the required civil documents and ensure you know how to obtain them. Also, make sure your petitioner has all necessary forms and information to prove they can financially support you.

Step 9: Upload and Submit Scanned Documents

Key Points:

1. Do Not Send Documents by Mail:

- You should not send any documents to the National Visa Center (NVC) by mail.
- However, it is crucial to bring all the civil documents you uploaded and submitted with your application to your visa interview.

2. How to Submit Documents:

- Log into the Consular Electronic Application Center (CEAC).

- Locate the “Start Now” buttons under Affidavit of Support Documents and Civil Documents.
- Upload all the required documents for each section.

3. Submission Process:

- The “Submit Documents” buttons will only become active after you have uploaded all required documents for each person involved in the application.
- Once you press “Submit Documents,” your case will be placed in line for review at the NV

Documentarily Complete

When the National Visa Center (NVC) determines that you have:

- Paid the necessary fees,
- Submitted the required immigrant visa application,
- Submitted the Affidavit of Support, and
- Submitted all supporting documents,

You will receive an email notification stating that your case is documentarily complete.

Next Steps:

1. **Scheduling an Interview:**

   - NVC will coordinate with the appropriate U.S. Embassy or Consulate to schedule your interview appointment.
   - NVC cannot predict the exact date when your interview will be scheduled, as it depends on the availability of appointment slots at the U.S. Embassy or Consulate.

2. **Appointment Scheduling Process**:

   - The U.S. Embassy or Consulate General informs NVC of the available interview dates.
   - NVC schedules interviews on a first-in, first-out basis, meaning cases are processed in the order they were completed.
   - If you are in a numerically limited (preference) visa category, your priority date must be current for you to receive an appointment.

3. **Tracking Your Priority Date:**

   - You can monitor the status of your priority date through the Visa Bulletin at https://usvisas.state.gov/visabulletin.

Make sure to keep an eye on your email for the notification that your case is documentarily complete and stay updated on your priority date to know when your interview may be scheduled.

What You Need to Complete and Submit Forms Online

For Immigrant Visa Applicants:

- Internet Access: Ensure you have a stable internet connection.
- NVC Case Number: You can find this in the message you received from the National Visa Center (NVC).
- Invoice I.D. Number: This is also provided in the message you received from NVC.

For Diversity Visa Applicants:

- Internet Access: A stable internet connection is required.
- Diversity Visa Case Number: This can be found in your selection notification on the [Diversity Visa Program website] (https://dvprogram.state.gov/).
- Principal Applicant's Date of Birth: Ensure you have the correct date of birth for the principal applicant.

Having these items ready will allow you to successfully complete and submit the necessary forms online for your visa application process.

General Requirements for Document Submission

1. Color Scanning:

    - If any document is in color, ensure that you scan it in color rather than black and white. This helps preserve the integrity and clarity of the document.

2. Scanning Both Sides:

    - For any document that has stamps, seals, or writing on the back, scan both the front and back sides.
    - Exception: If the back of the document is blank, you do not need to scan it.

3. Certified Translations:

    - If you have a certified translation of a document, include the translation along with the original (foreign language) document.
    - Both the translation and the original document should be scanned and saved in a single file.

Instructions

1. Emails and U.S. Embassy Information:

   - All the necessary email addresses and U.S. Embassy details are included in the Study Guide Book. Use these resources when requesting a case transfer.

2. After the Case is Transferred:

   - Once your case has been transferred, you need to create an account on https://www.ustraveldocs.com/.

3. Selecting the Appropriate Country:

   - During the account creation process, you must select the country where your case will be processed.
   - Example: For cases being processed in the Dominican Republic, select "Dominican Republic" from the list of countries, and then proceed to create your profile.

4. Refer to Examples:

   - Detailed examples and further instructions on how to create the account and select the appropriate country are provided in the Study Guide Book. Follow these examples to ensure accuracy.

Here's a draft of the letter for requesting an expedited interview:

[Your Name]
[Your Address]
[City, State, ZIP Code]
[Email Address]
[Phone Number]
[Date]

To Whom It May Concern,

I am writing to urgently request an expedited interview for my [fiancé(e)/spouse/relative/etc.]. Due to the increasingly dangerous situation in Haiti, I have had to move them to the Dominican Republic, even though it is also not entirely safe due to the ongoing political tensions between the two countries.

My priority date for this case has been since [Insert Priority Date]. Given the dire circumstances, I am pleading for this case to be expedited at the earliest possible convenience.

Thank you for your understanding and prompt attention to this matter.

Sincerely,

[Your Name]

HOW TO SEND THE INQUIRY TO NVC FOR YOUR CLIENT MAKE SURE YOU ENTER THE BEFICIARY INFORMATION

https://travel.state.gov/content/travel/en/us-visas/visa-information-resources/ask-nvc.html?wcmmode=disabled

Public Inquiry Form

Inquiry Response Time

NVC response times to public inquiries continue to be lengthy. We ask that you make a subsequent inquiry only if you do not receive a response within our published timeframes.

Interviews

The U.S. Embassy or Consulate tells NVC which dates they are holding interviews. NVC fills these appointments on a first-in, first-out basis and cannot predict when an interview will be scheduled.

Once complete, your case will remain at NVC until an appointment is scheduled, at which time we will send it to the appropriate U.S. Embassy or Consulate. We will notify the applicant, petitioner, and attorney (if applicable) when an appointment is scheduled.

Case status

For the most up-to-date case status, please log into the Consular Electronic Application Center (CEAC).

Last contact date

To update the last contact date for cases actively processing at NVC, please continue to pay fees and submit the required documents by logging into the Consular Electronic Application Center (CEAC).

Note: Responses to inquiries through the NVC Public Inquiry form will come from TSGSystem@tsg.state.gov. Please do not send inquiries directly to that address as they will not be received by the National Visa Center. Send all inquiries using the below Public Inquiry Form.

Date of Birth formatting: please note that the date of birth on this form must be submitted following the (dd/Month/yyyy) format. For example: 01/June/1990.

This will be three letters, followed by ten numbers, For example: ABC2014123456

NVC Case Number or USCIS Receipt Number:(required)

This is the person who is going to immigrate to the United States. Please enter the name as it appears on his or her passport.

Principal Applicant's Full Name:(required)

Date of birth must be entered following the (dd/Month/yyyy) format. For example: 01/June/1990.

Please enter the date of birth as it appears on the Principal Applicant's passport. If the passport does not show a day, choose the first of the month. If the passport does not show a month, choose January.

Principal Applicant's Date of Birth:(required)

This is the person who is sponsoring the Principal Applicant. Please enter the name as it appears on his or her passport.

Petitioner's Full Name:(required)
Who are you?(required)
Select an Identity...
Petitioner

Principal Applicant
Attorney of Record
Other
Your Email Address:(required)

Important! Please double-check your email address. We can't write back to you without it!

Enter Your Inquiry Below:(required)

This will be three letters, followed by ten numbers, For example: ABC2014123456

NVC Case Number or USCIS Receipt Number: (required)

This is the person who is going to immigrate to the United States. Please enter the name as it appears on his or her passport.

Principal Applicant's Full Name: (required)

Date of birth must be entered following the (dd/Month/yyyy) format. For example: 01/June/1990.

Please enter the date of birth as it appears on the Principal Applicant's passport. If the passport does not show a day, choose the first of the month. If the passport does not show a month, choose January.

Principal Applicant's Date of Birth: (required) dd/Month/yyyy

This is the person who is sponsoring the Principal Applicant. Please enter the name as it appears on his or her passport.

Petitioner's Full Name: (required)

Who are you? (required) Select an Identity...

Your Email Address: (required) example@domain

Important! Please double-check your email address. We can't write back to you without it!

Important! Please double-check your email address. We can't write back to you without it!

Enter Your Inquiry Below: (required)

Attachments: (Max. 5)

Choose File No file chosen

Add More Files

CAPTCHA Validation:

I'm not a robot

reCAPTCHA

Privacy - Terms

Reset Submit

Pay your visa fees

Visa applicants, including children, are required to pay a non-refundable, non-transferable visa application fee, sometimes referred to as the MRV fee, before applying for a nonimmigrant visa. The visa application fee must be paid whether a visa is issued or not. The type of visa for which you apply determines the fee amount. This webpage lists visa application fees associated with each nonimmigrant visa type. Please note that only the application fees for nonimmigrant visas are listed here.

Visa types and application fee amounts

Visa types and application fee amounts

Exchange Rate
Current Consular Exchange Rate: 60 DOP = 1 USD Current Rate Valid Through: 2024-08-31

Visa types	Visa types	Visa types	Visa types
B Business/Tourist **C-1** Transit **D** Ship/Airline Crew **F** Student (academic) **I** Journalist and Media **J** Exchange Visitors **M** Student (vocational) **T**	**CW** Transitional Worker CNMI **H** Temporary/Seasonal Workers and Employment, Trainees **L** Intercompany Transferees **O** Person with Extraordinary Ability **P** Atheletes, Artists,	**E** Treaty Trader/Investor,Australian Professional Speciality,Long-Term Investor CNMI	**K** Fiancé(e) or Spouse of U.S. Citizen

$185	$205	$315	$265
11100.00 DOP	12300.00 DOP	18900.00 DOP	15900.00 DOP
Non-refundable	Non-refundable	Non-refundable	Non-refundable

Visa types and conditions with no fee required

Fee Payment Options

Cash at bank

Online payment with Banco Popular Bank

Online payment with a Credit Card or Debit Card (Check/Bank Card)

Bank and payment options/pay my visa fee

Apply for a U.S. Visa (ustraveldocs.com)

How to apply for nonimmigrant visa

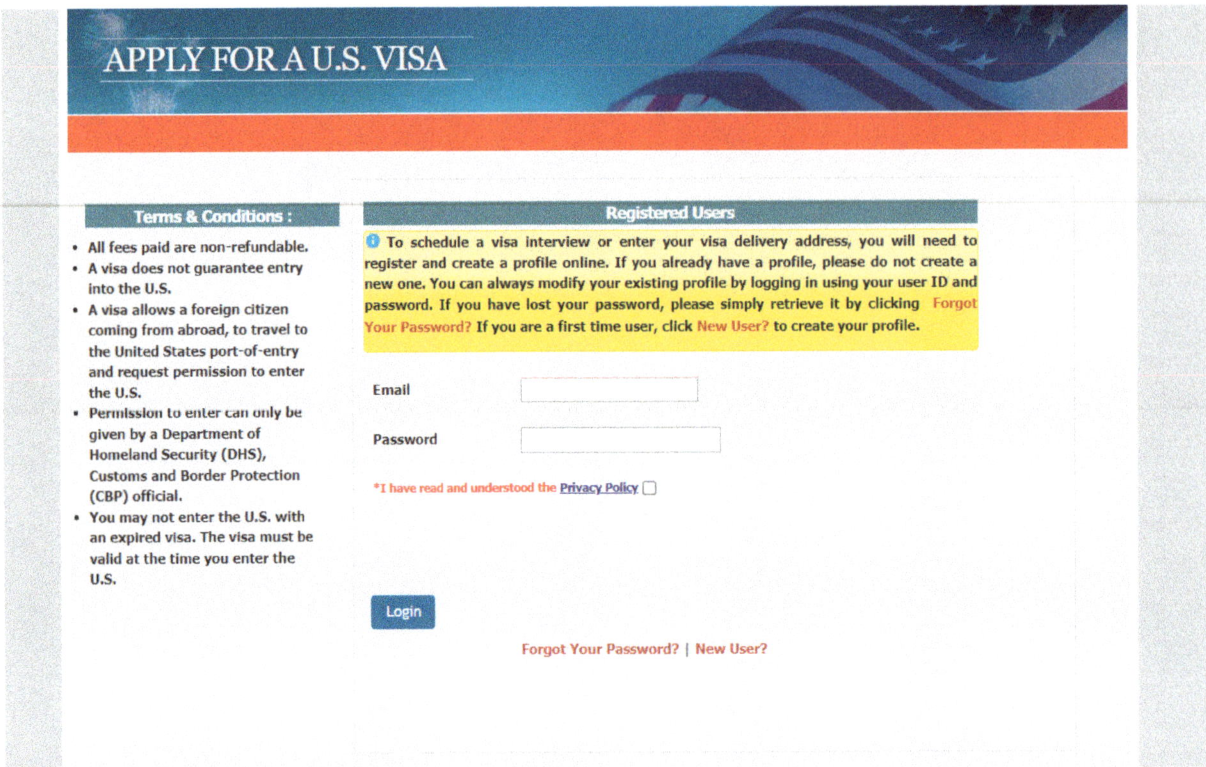

APPLY FOR A U.S. VISA

Terms & Conditions :

- All fees paid are non-refundable.
- A visa does not guarantee entry into the U.S.
- A visa allows a foreign citizen coming from abroad, to travel to the United States port-of-entry and request permission to enter the U.S.
- Permission to enter can only be given by a Department of Homeland Security (DHS), Customs and Border Protection (CBP) official.
- You may not enter the U.S. with an expired visa. The visa must be valid at the time you enter the U.S.

Registered Users

To schedule a visa interview or enter your visa delivery address, you will need to register and create a profile online. If you already have a profile, please do not create a new one. You can always modify your existing profile by logging in using your user ID and password. If you have lost your password, please simply retrieve it by clicking Forgot Your Password? If you are a first time user, click New User? to create your profile.

Email

Password

*I have read and understood the Privacy Policy

Login

Forgot Your Password? | New User?

CREATE THE PROFILE PLEASE MAKE SURE YOU PICK THE RIGHT COUNTRY

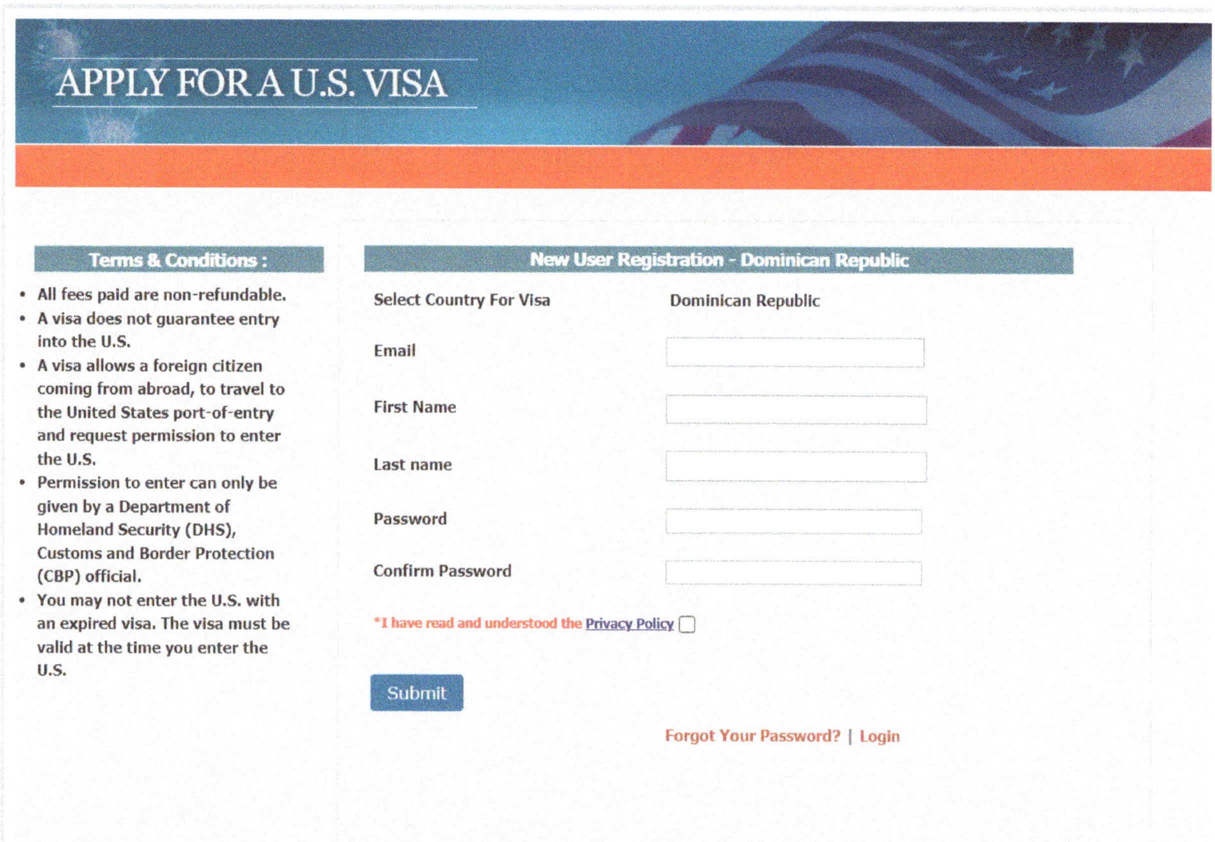

Check visa application status

If you are a nonimmigrant applicant, you may check your DS-160 and visa application status online by entering your interview location and your DS-160 barcode number in the page linked below.

Track my passport by telephone

+1(829) 956-5144

Callers in the United States

+1(703) 988-3410

1. Send an email to passportstatus@ustraveldocs.com
2. In the subject and/or body enter only a valid passport number exactly as it was entered at the time the appointment was scheduled.
3. Do not enter any additional text. You will receive an automatic response with the status.

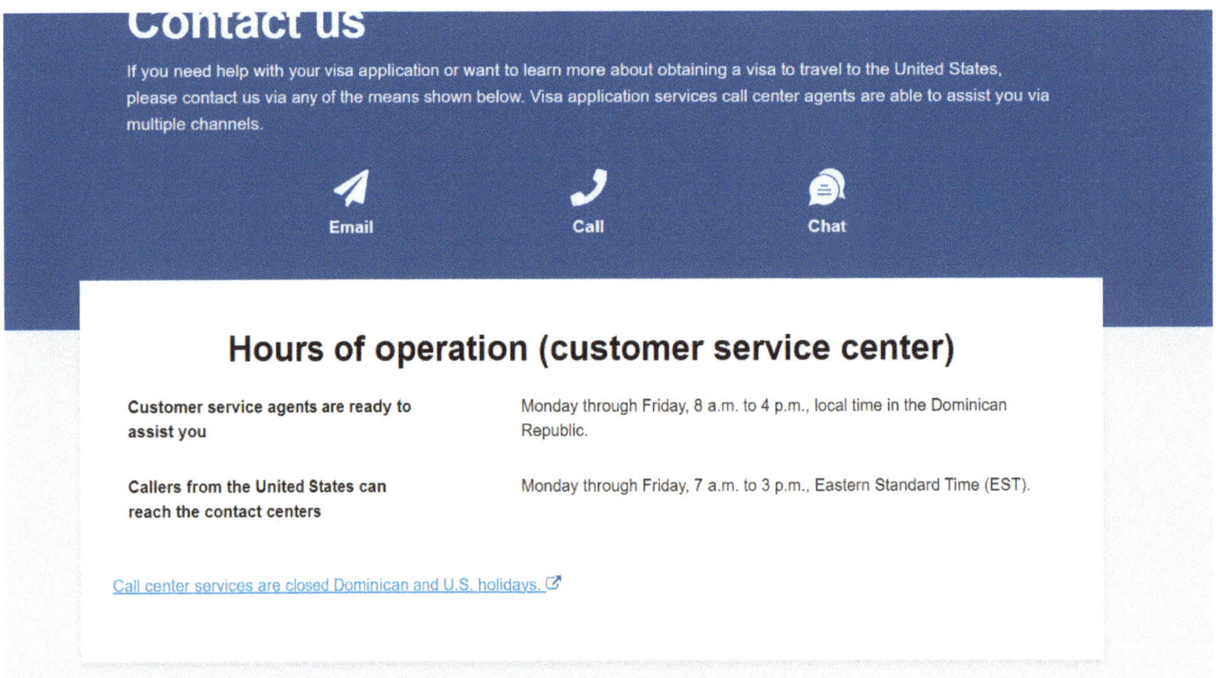

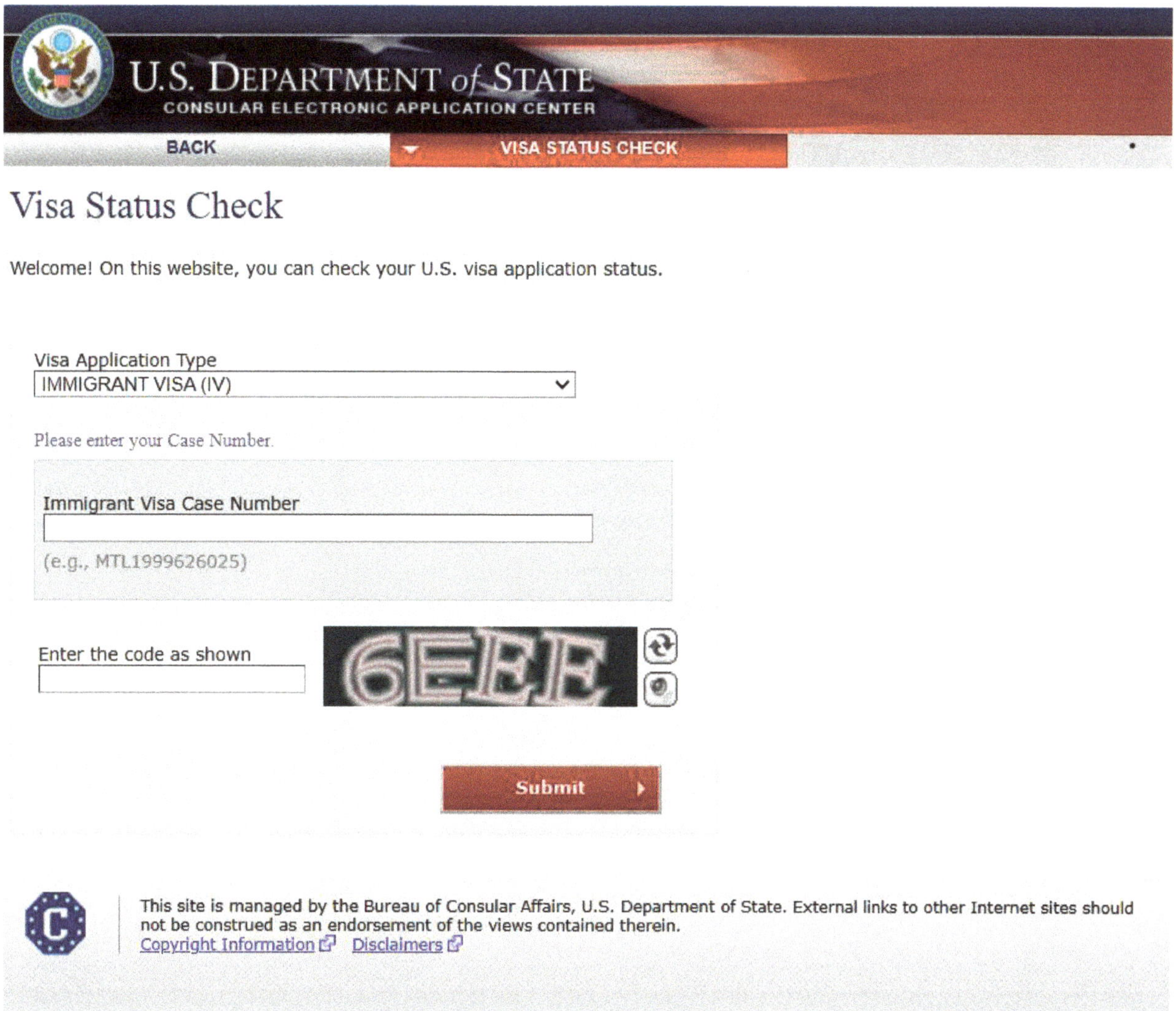
U.S. DEPARTMENT of STATE
CONSULAR ELECTRONIC APPLICATION CENTER
BACK
VISA STATUS CHECK
Visa Status Check
Welcome! On this website, you can check your U.S. visa application status.
Visa Application Type
IMMIGRANT VISA (IV)
Please enter your Case Number.
Immigrant Visa Case Number
(e.g., MTL1999626025)
Enter the code as shown
6EEE
Submit
This site is managed by the Bureau of Consular Affairs, U.S. Department of State. External links to other Internet sites should not be construed as an endorsement of the views contained therein.
Copyright Information
Disclaimers

Consular Electronic Application Center (state.gov)

Immigrant Visa - Sign In (state.gov)

Contact Us

U.S. DEPARTMENT of STATE
CONSULAR ELECTRONIC APPLICATION CENTER

Immigrant Visa

Sign In

Welcome to the Consular Electronic Application Center – Immigrant/Diversity Visa portal. To access your case, please enter your case number below.

Please do not use the browser's back or refresh buttons while using the CEAC site. Instead, use the navigation links on the page. You will lose information if you use the browser's back or refresh button, and will need to log back into the application.

Privacy Act

AUTHORITIES: The information sought is pursuant to 8 U.S.C. §§ 1201-1202.

PURPOSE: The information solicited on this form will be used by consular officers to determine an applicant's eligibility for a visa.

ROUTINE USES: The information on this form may be shared with federal, state, and local government agencies, members of Congress, and officials of foreign governments in accordance with certain approved routine uses. More information on the Routine Uses for the system can be found in the System of Records Notice State-39, Visa Records.

DISCLOSURE: Although providing this information is voluntary, failure to provide the information requested on this form may result in the applicant's inability to receive an immigrant or nonimmigrant visa.

☐ I have read the terms of the Privacy Act Notice

Case Number

Continue

Important: Before You Begin

Browser Requirements

**Please be patient.

Step 9: Upload and Submit Scanned Documents

IMPORTANT: Do not send any documents to NVC by mail. However, you must bring every civil document you uploaded and submitted with your application to your visa interview.

To submit documents, log into CEAC and go to the "Start Now" buttons located under *Affidavit of Support Documents* and *Civil Documents*. When you have uploaded all the required documents for each section, press "Submit Documents". The "Submit Documents" buttons will not work unless you have uploaded all of the required documents for each person. Once you press "Submit Documents", your case will be placed in line for review at the National Visa Center (NVC).

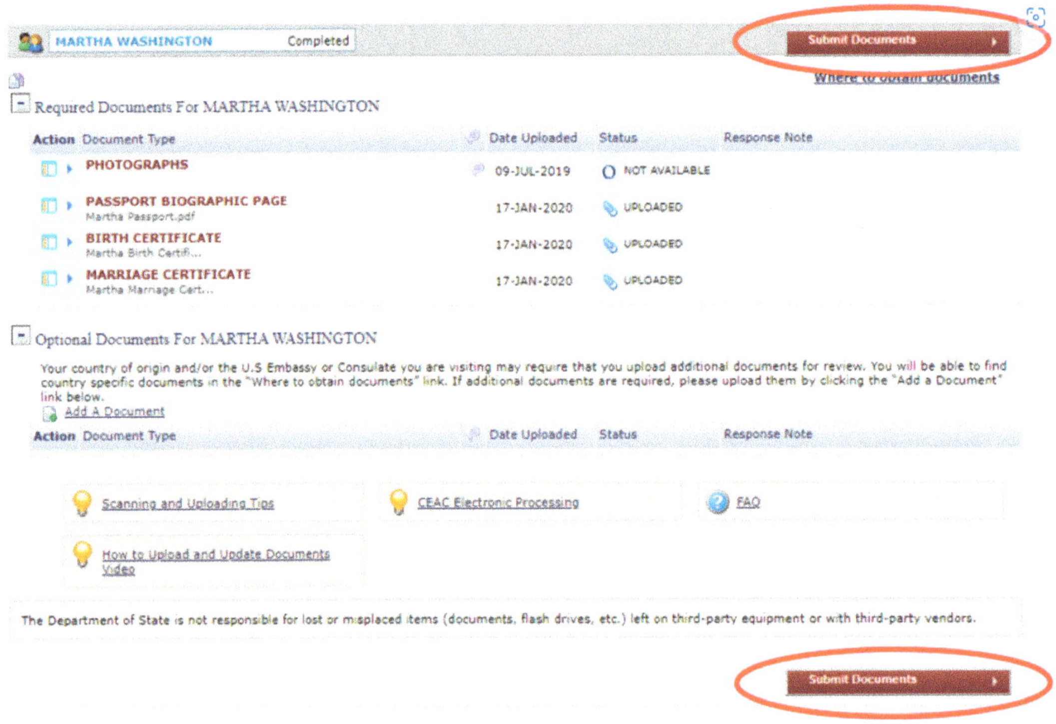

Online Nonimmigrant Visa Application (DS-160)

Apply For a Nonimmigrant Visa

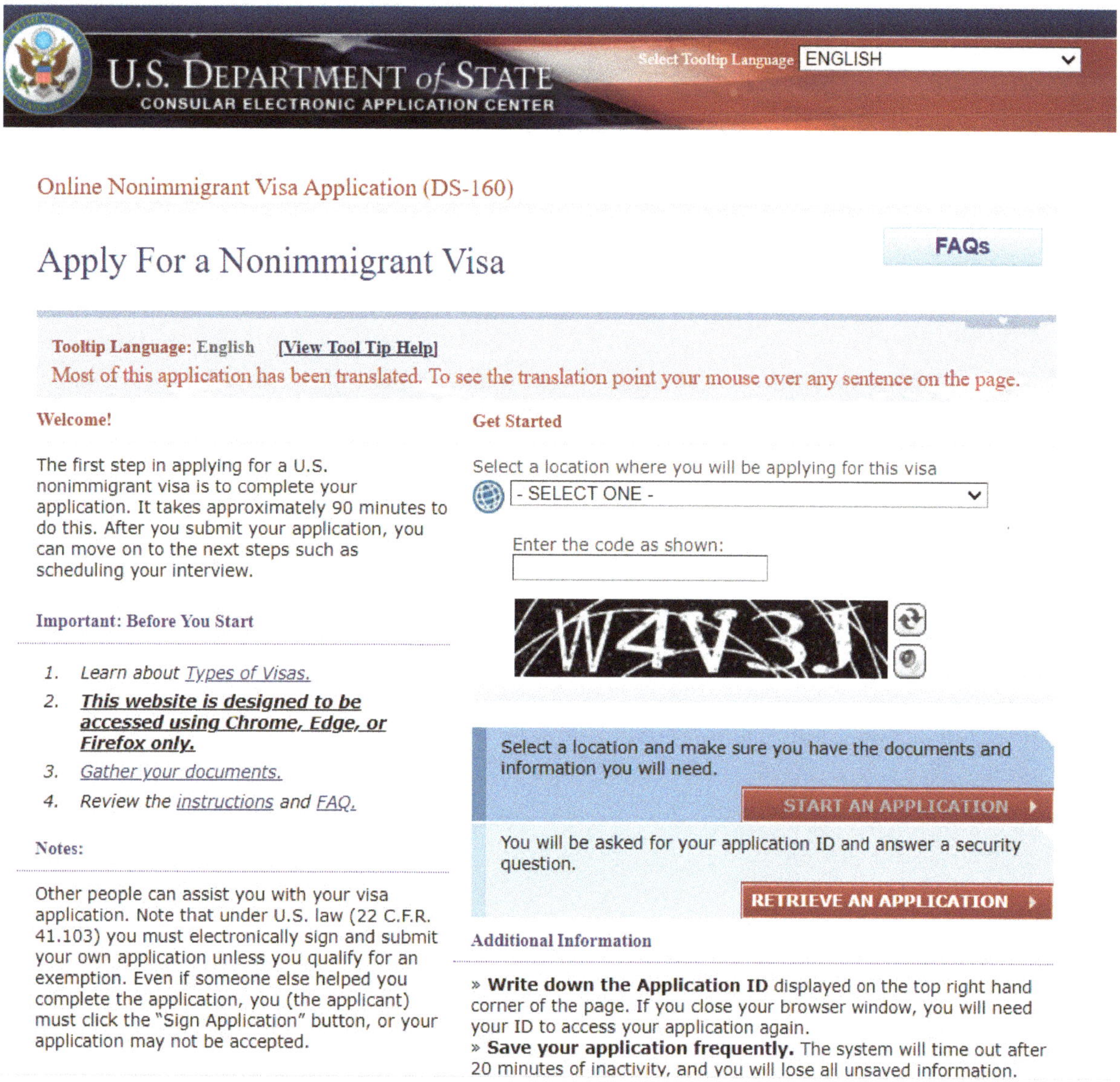

U.S. DEPARTMENT of STATE
CONSULAR ELECTRONIC APPLICATION CENTER

Select Tooltip Language ENGLISH

Online Nonimmigrant Visa Application (DS-160)

Apply For a Nonimmigrant Visa

FAQs

Tooltip Language: English [View Tool Tip Help]

Most of this application has been translated. To see the translation point your mouse over any sentence on the page.

Welcome!

The first step in applying for a U.S. nonimmigrant visa is to complete your application. It takes approximately 90 minutes to do this. After you submit your application, you can move on to the next steps such as scheduling your interview.

Important: Before You Start

1. *Learn about Types of Visas.*
2. ***This website is designed to be accessed using Chrome, Edge, or Firefox only.***
3. *Gather your documents.*
4. *Review the instructions and FAQ.*

Notes:

Other people can assist you with your visa application. Note that under U.S. law (22 C.F.R. 41.103) you must electronically sign and submit your own application unless you qualify for an exemption. Even if someone else helped you complete the application, you (the applicant) must click the "Sign Application" button, or your application may not be accepted.

Get Started

Select a location where you will be applying for this visa

- SELECT ONE -

Enter the code as shown:

Select a location and make sure you have the documents and information you will need.

START AN APPLICATION

You will be asked for your application ID and answer a security question.

RETRIEVE AN APPLICATION

Additional Information

» **Write down the Application ID** displayed on the top right hand corner of the page. If you close your browser window, you will need your ID to access your application again.

» **Save your application frequently.** The system will time out after 20 minutes of inactivity, and you will lose all unsaved information.

Step 8: Scan Collected Documents

Once you have collected all the necessary documents, you must scan and save them.

In order to scan your documents, you will need access to a computer and scanner or a smartphone with an internet connection. If you do not have access to these, common places with this type of equipment are libraries, community centers, internet cafés, and copy shops. Note: If you choose to use a public computer, be sure to delete your scanned documents once you have finished uploading them.

Unless specifically directed to do so by the National Visa Center (NVC) please do not mail any documents to NVC. If you do, you will delay the processing of your case and risk losing any documents you send.

In order to ensure your case does not experience delays in processing, follow these guidelines when scanning your documents:

Step 10: Prepare for the Interview

After the National Visa Center (NVC) schedules your visa interview appointment, they will send you, your petitioner, and your agent/attorney (if applicable) an email noting the appointment date and time. **After you receive an interview Appointment Letter from NVC, you must take the following steps BEFORE the interview date.**

1. Schedule and Complete a Medical Examination

You (and each family member or "derivative applicant" applying for a visa with you) are required to schedule a medical appointment with an authorized physician in the country where you will be interviewed. This exam must be with an embassy-approved doctor, also referred to as the Panel Physician. **Exams conducted by other physicians will not be accepted.** The exam results can take up to 96 hours. You must complete your medical examination, along with any required vaccinations, before your scheduled visa interview date. Please visit our List of U.S. Embassies and Consulates for country-specific medical examination instructions.

After your exam, the Panel Physician will either send the exam results directly to the embassy or give you a sealed envelope. If the doctor gives you an envelope, do not open it. Instead, bring it to your visa interview and give it to the consular officer.

2. Register for Courier Service/Other Pre-Interview Instructions

3. Gather Documents Required for the Interview

Every visa applicant, no matter their age, must bring certain documents to the interview, including photographs, and the original or certified copy version of all civil documents submitted to NVC. You **do not** need to bring your Affidavit of Support or financial evidence you submitted to NVC.

What happens if you forget to bring something on this list? The consular officer will not be able to complete the processing of your visa. You will have to gather the missing items and provide them to the embassy or consulate, and may have to come for additional interviews. **Failure to bring all items on the above list can delay visa issuance.**

Step 11: Applicant Interview

Prior to the interview, ensure you have followed the U.S. Embassy or Consulate interview preparation instructions.

On the scheduled date and time of your interview appointment, go to the U.S. Embassy or Consulate with your printed visa application (DS-260) confirmation page. A consular officer will interview you (and accompanying family member beneficiaries) and determine whether or not you are eligible to receive an immigrant visa. As part of the interview process, ink-free, digital fingerprint scans will be taken.

Important Notice

You should not make permanent financial commitments, such as selling your house, car or property, resigning from your job, or making other travel arrangements, until you have received your immigrant visa.

Who Must Attend the Interview

- You (the principal applicant), regardless of age.
- Any family members immigrating with you, if they will be at least 14 years old on the day of the interview. These family members include your spouse and any qualified unmarried children on the same petition and case number.
- Any family member, regardless of age, who has their own petition/case number. That's because they are their own principal applicant.

Who Is Not Required to Attend the interview

- Your family members under the age of 14 on the day of the interview, even if they are noted as traveling applicants on the Interview Appointment Letter you receive from the National Visa Center (NVC).
- Your family members (spouse and/or qualified unmarried children) who will immigrate at a later date and travel separately from you. They will be scheduled for a separate interview appointment. You should contact the U.S. Embassy or Consulate directly to arrange separate interviews, if needed.

- Your sponsor/petitioner.

Even though they don't have to attend the interview, these family members are usually still welcome to come with you. Many consular officers appreciate this opportunity to see the whole family together, which may reduce follow-up questions later. Please check if there are specific instructions from the consular section where you will interview.

What to bring to the Interview

The applicant is responsible to bring all required original or certified copy civil documents to the visa interview. Failure to bring all required documents to the interview may cause delay or denial of the visa. You must bring the following documents to the interview:

- **Appointment Letter** – The interview appointment letter you received from NVC.
- **Passport** – For each applicant, an unexpired passport valid for six months beyond the intended date of entry into the United States
- **Photographs** – two identical color photograph(s) for each applicant, which must meet the general Photograph Requirements.
- **DS-260 Confirmation Page**
- **Supporting Documents** – original or certified copies of all civil documents you uploaded into CEAC.

Your original documents will be returned to you when the interview has been completed. Any photocopies provided may be kept.

- **English Translations** – If documents requiring English translation were not sent to NVC, you must obtain them and present them on the day of your interview. For more information please review the U.S. Embassy or Consulate interview preparation instructions.
- **Visa Fees** – If your visa application fees were collected by NVC, you do not need to pay again. However, if you or any family member did not pay all the necessary fees, you will be asked to pay any unpaid fees at the U.S. Embassy or Consulate.

Failure to Appear for Interview - If you cannot appear at your scheduled interview, contact the U.S. Embassy or Consulate as soon as possible. If you do not contact the U.S. Embassy or Consulate within one year of receiving your interview appointment letter, your case may be terminated and your immigrant visa petition cancelled, and any fees paid will not be refunded.

Step 12: After the Interview

Important Notice

Do not sell your house, car or property, resign from your job, or make non-refundable flight or other travel arrangements, until you have received your immigrant visa.

If your visa is approved, you will be informed how and when your passport and visa will be returned to you.

Passport and Visa

Your immigrant visa will be placed on a page in your passport. Please review the printed information right away to make sure there are no errors. If there are any spelling or biographical errors, contact the embassy or consulate immediately.

What do I need to do before I travel?

You must pay the USCIS Immigrant Fee to U.S. Citizenship and Immigration Services (USCIS) after you receive your immigrant visa and before you travel to the United States. Only children who enter the United States under the Orphan or Hague adoption programs, Iraqi and Afghan special immigrants, returning residents (SB-1s), and those issued K visas are exempt from this fee. Please visit the USCIS website for more information and to pay the fee.

Please Note: USCIS will not issue a Permanent Resident Card (Form I-551 or Green Card) until you have paid the fee.

When should I travel?

You must arrive in and apply for admission to the United States no later than the visa expiration date printed on your visa. An immigrant visa is usually valid for up to six months from the date of issuance unless your medical examination expires sooner, which may make your visa valid for less than six months.

Entering the United States

When traveling to the United States, the primary (or principal) applicant must enter before or at the same time as derivative family members with visas. A visa does not guarantee entry into the United States. The Department of Homeland Security, U.S. Customs and Border Protection (CBP) officials have authority to grant or deny admission. Learn about admission and entry requirements on the CBP website. When you are admitted, you will enter as a Lawful Permanent Resident, also called a green card holder, and will be permitted to work and live in the United States.

When You are a Permanent Resident – Learn more about your status as a Lawful Permanent Resident. You may also wish to review Welcome to the United States: A Guide for New Immigrants.

Social Security Number – To learn about the U.S. Social Security Administration benefits available to Legal Permanent Residents, and how to apply for a social security number card, visit the Social Security Administration website.

If your visa is denied, you will be informed by the consular officer why you are ineligible to receive a visa. Based on U.S. law, not everyone who applies is qualified or eligible for a visa to come to the United States. Under U.S. law, many factors could make an applicant ineligible to receive a visa. For more information, please refer to Ineligibilities for U.S. Visas. In some instances, the law might allow you to apply for a waiver of the ineligibility. If you are able to apply for such a waiver, the consular officer will advise you on the steps to take. Please review the Visa Denials webpage for more detailed information.

In some situations the consular officer does not have sufficient information needed to conclude that the visa applicant established eligibility for the visa sought. In those cases, the officer must refuse the visa application, and will do so under section 221(g) of the Immigration and Nationality Act. If the reason you were unable to establish eligibility relates to a missing supporting documentation, then the consular officer will inform you if information or documents are missing and how to provide it.

Administrative Processing

Some visa applications refused under 221(g) of the Immigration and Nationality Act may require further administrative processing. When administrative processing is required, the consular officer will inform the applicant at the end of the interview. The duration of the administrative processing will vary based on the individual circumstances of each case. While the case is in administrative processing, the application must remain refused as the applicant has not established eligibility for the visa sought. At the conclusion of the administrative processing period, the consular officer may conclude that an applicant is now qualified for the visa for which he or she applied. The officer may also conclude that the applicant remains ineligible for a visa.

Except in cases of emergency travel (i.e. serious illnesses, injuries, or deaths in your immediate family), before making inquiries about status of administrative processing, applicants should wait at least 180 days from the date of interview or submission of supplemental documents, whichever is later.

www.ingramcontent.com/pod-product-compliance
Lightning Source LLC
Chambersburg PA
CBHW041512210926
51847CB00011B/124